# Discover
# How Stuff
# Works

Illustrations Copyright © 2004 Orpheus Books Ltd
2 Church Green, Witney, Oxon OX28 4AW

Illustrated by Peter Dennis (Linda Rogers Associates)

Text and Design Copyright © 2005, 2006 Reading Challenge, Inc.
www.readingchallenge.com

Manufactured in China

0606-2HH

**Visit us at www.readingchallenge.com**

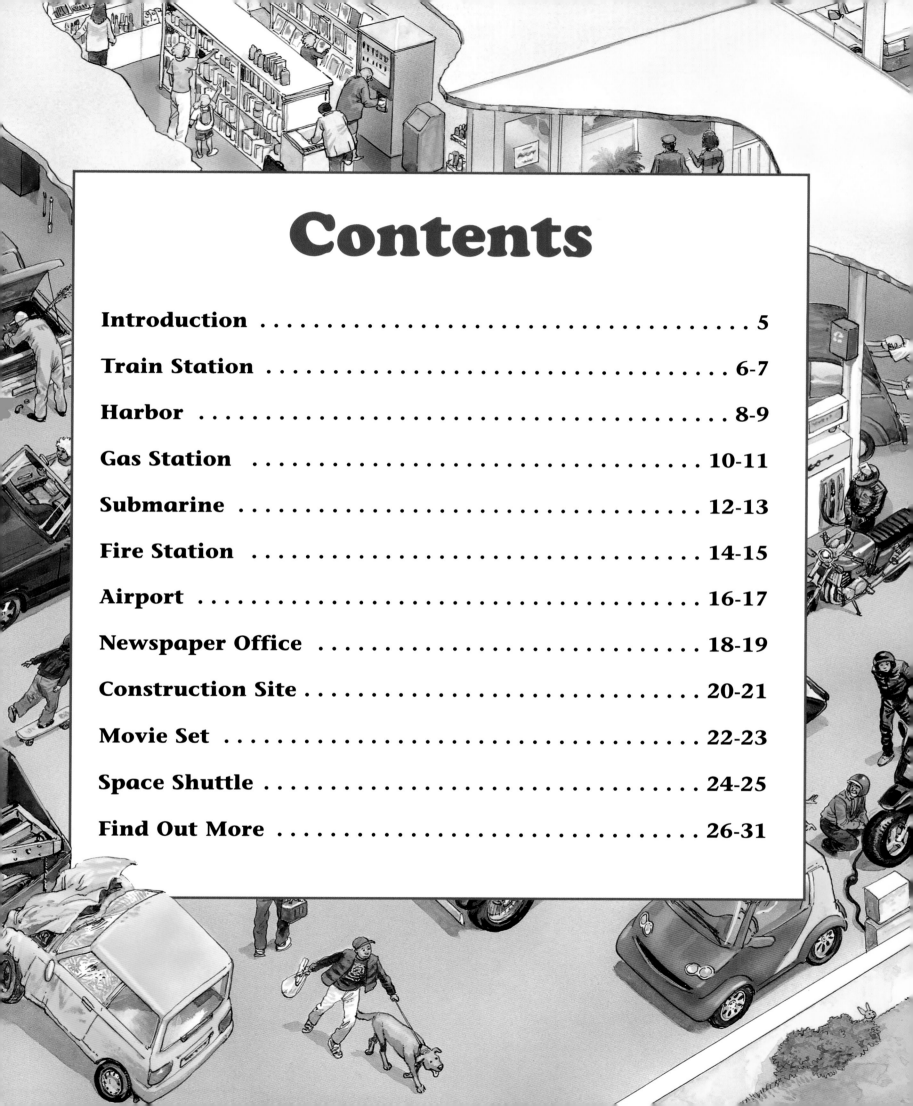

# Contents

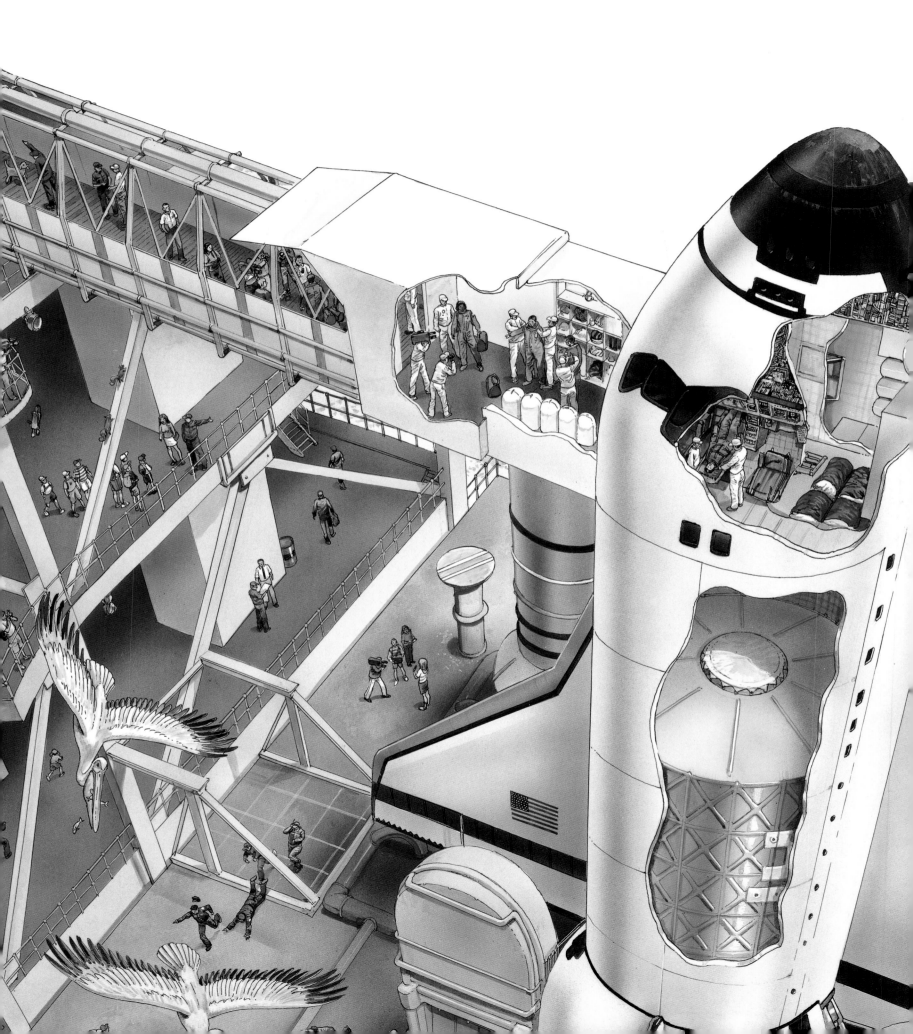

# Introduction

Imagine being an astronaut about to blast off into outer space, or a firefighter battling a raging blaze. What would you see? How would you feel? What would you do?

**HOW STUFF WORKS** is a wonderfully illustrated book about the inner workings of many interesting places, including a submarine, a train station, and a movie set. In each section, there is a fun search-and-find activity to help you identify the important things and people who help make stuff work.

The **Find Out More** section in the back of this book is packed with facts, trivia, and interesting websites for you to explore.

So put on your thinking cap and get ready to
**Read, Search & Find**™ as you
**Discover**
**HOW STUFF WORKS!**

# Train Station

A train station is a very busy place. To ride on a train, you must first buy a ticket. A large screen tells you what time your train will leave and where it will be. Some people arrive early and sit and wait for their trains. Others get to the station late and have to hurry.

## Search & Find

- ☐ Brooms (2)
- ☐ Children dancing
- ☐ Dogs (3)
- ☐ Guitar case
- ☐ People reading newspapers (4)
- ☐ People using cell phones (5)
- ☐ Scooter
- ☐ Taxi

### Platform
A platform is where people get on and off the train. Friends and family stand on the platform to wave hello or good-bye.

### Electric cart
Electric carts transport people and luggage around the station. The carts travel slowly and are very quiet.

### Engineer
The engineer drives the train.

### Information booth
Travelers can get a train schedule (SKEH-jool) and other information about trains here.

### Buying a ticket
People wait in line to buy their tickets. They can buy them from a ticket seller or a machine.

### Conductor
The conductor signals the engineer that everyone is aboard. He also collects and sells tickets on the train.

**Find Out More** on page 26

# Harbor

A harbor is a place where ships and boats dock. Workers load and unload products from cargo ships. Fishing boats bring in the day's catch. Sailboats and yachts stay in a harbor when they are not traveling the seas. Ferries take people and their cars to places across the water. A lighthouse stands at the entrance to the harbor and serves as a guide for the boats.

## Search & Find

- [ ] Artist
- [ ] Bicycles (2)
- [ ] Cats (2)
- [ ] Flags (2)
- [ ] Hammock
- [ ] Life preservers (3)
- [ ] Skateboarders
- [ ] Telescope

## Seagull
Seagulls live near the sea. They like to eat fish, but will eat anything they can find.

## Kayak
A kayak (KYE-ak) is a small boat. Some kayaks can hold two people.

## Fishing boat
People use special boats to go out and catch large amounts of fish. Ice keeps the fish fresh until the boat returns to port. Sometimes, part of the catch is sold at the harbor.

## Jet Ski
A jet ski is a fast and fun way to ride on water.

## Lighthouse
A lighthouse shines a very powerful beam of light. This lighthouse guides sailors into the harbor at night.

## Fishing
Some people catch fish to eat. This boy goes fishing just for fun.

## Shipping container
Things sent across the ocean are loaded into shipping containers. The containers are stacked like giant building blocks on board the cargo ship.

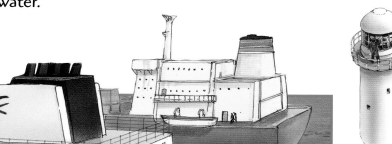

**Find Out More** on page 27

9

# Gas Station

People go to a gas station to get fuel for their cars, trucks, and motorcycles. A fuel truck pumps gasoline into storage tanks. Mechanics (mih-KAN-iks) fix cars in the garage. Some people go there to fill their tires with air. Others go to get their cars washed. This gas station has a store that sells snacks.

## Search & Find

- [ ] Cat
- [ ] Convertible cars (2)
- [ ] Dogs (4)
- [ ] Go-cart
- [ ] In-line skaters (2)
- [ ] Scooter
- [ ] Sheep (5)
- [ ] Skateboards (3)

**Find Out More**
on page 27

### Motorcycle
Motorcycles run on gas, just like cars and trucks.

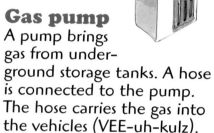

### Gas pump
A pump brings gas from underground storage tanks. A hose is connected to the pump. The hose carries the gas into the vehicles (VEE-uh-kulz).

### Classic car
A classic car is an old car. Classic cars are often seen at car shows.

### Bicycles
Bicycles run on people power, instead of gas. But some people might bring their bike to the gas station to fill the tires with air.

### Mechanic
Mechanics know a lot about how cars work. They can fix cars that have problems.

### Car wash
Some people bring their cars to the car wash. Giant rollers and a strong spray of water are used to clean them. A powerful blower dries the cars on the way out.

### Car waxing
Waxing a car helps keep it shiny and clean. The wax helps protect the car from rust.

11

# Submarine

A submarine is built to travel under the sea. Some can stay underwater for months at a time. Hundreds of people can live on a submarine. Each member of the crew has a special job to do. Some members work in the control room. Others take turns working in the kitchen. Smaller submarines are used to explore the ocean depths.

## Search & Find

- ☐ Cook
- ☐ Fire extinguishers (3)
- ☐ Giant squid
- ☐ Octopus
- ☐ Shower
- ☐ Whale
- ☐ Spotlights (6)

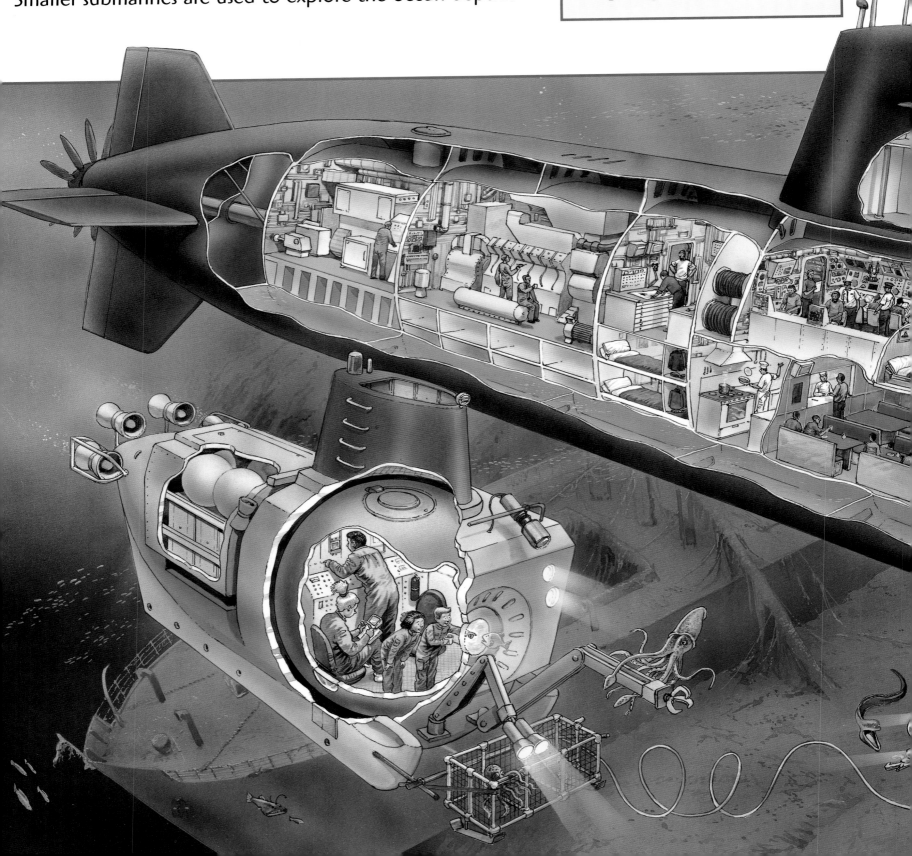

## Submersible

A submersible (sub-MUR-suh-bul) is a small submarine used by explorers or people doing research. It allows them to see places and sea creatures that a large submarine cannot.

## Probe

A probe is a small craft attached to the submersible. It can explore even deeper into the water.

## Control room

The captain, with the help of the crew, runs the submarine from the control room. The computers and other machines needed to operate the sub are located here.

## Captain's quarters

The captain is in charge of the crew. Captains sleep in their own cabin.

## Galley

The kitchen on a submarine is called a galley. This is where the cook works.

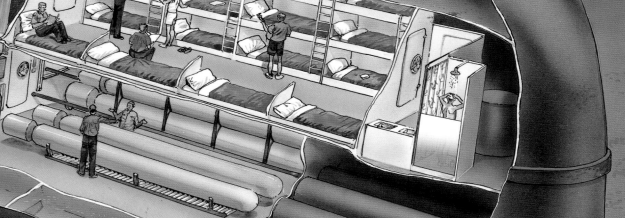

## Crew's quarters

Space is tight on a submarine. The crew's bunk beds are stacked on top of one another in the same room.

**Find Out More** on page 28

# Fire Station

Firefighters must always be ready for a fire. When the alarm sounds, they quickly put on their uniforms. They hop into their trucks. Then they rush to the fire. Some firefighters rescue people trapped inside the burning building. Others put out the fire with water from the hoses.

## Search & Find

- ☐ Axes (3)
- ☐ Birdcage
- ☐ Cats (2)
- ☐ Computers (3)
- ☐ Slippers
- ☐ Soccer player
- ☐ Teddy bear
- ☐ Tricycle

## Firefighter
A firefighter is a brave person who puts out fires and rescues people.

## Putting out the fire
Firefighters spray water onto a fire to put it out. Long ladders help the firefighters reach the flames.

## Treating injuries
Sometimes people get hurt in a fire. They receive special care for their injuries.

## Rescue
A firefighter's number-one job is to rescue people who are trapped in a burning building.

## Safety mat
Sometimes, people who are trapped in a building can escape by jumping onto a safety mat. The mat gives them a soft landing.

**Find Out More**
on page 28

# Airport

The airport is a very busy place. It is full of people who are traveling from one place to another. There are also many workers at an airport. They help the travelers and make sure everyone is safe.

## Search & Find

- [ ] Coffee shop
- [ ] Dog
- [ ] Elevator
- [ ] Fuel truck
- [ ] Man on crutches
- [ ] Skateboard
- [ ] Sunglasses stand
- [ ] TV monitor

### Luggage
Suitcases and bags are called luggage.

### Check-in desk
The check-in desk is the first stop for travelers. Here, they drop off their luggage and get boarding passes. The boarding pass is what allows each person to get on the plane.

### Control tower

Air-traffic controllers work in the control tower. From there, they direct the airplanes that are landing and taking off.

### Metal detector
The metal detector helps airport workers make sure that no dangerous items are brought onboard the planes.

### Baggage-claim area
At the end of a flight, travelers go to the baggage-claim area to pick up their luggage.

### Flight attendant
A flight attendant takes care of passengers on a plane.

**Find Out More** on page 29

# Newspaper Office

It takes many people to make a newspaper. Reporters write articles. Editors decide which stories to publish. Photographers take pictures. When they finish putting the paper together, a huge machine prints it. Then workers load copies onto delivery trucks.

## Search & Find

- [ ] Cat
- [ ] Cell phone
- [ ] Fire extinguishers
- [ ] Magnifying glass
- [ ] Mice (2)
- [ ] Ruler
- [ ] Spilled coffee
- [ ] Wastepaper baskets (2)

### Forklift
A forklift is a small truck that uses steel forks to lift and carry heavy things.

### Print operator
The print operator is the person who runs the big machine that prints the newspapers.

### Courier
A courier (KUR-ee-ur) is a person who delivers packages or mail.

## Reporter

Reporters gather information. Then they write about what they have learned.

## School tour

Students on a school tour learn what happens at a newspaper office.

## Photographer

A news photographer takes pictures that will be used in the paper.

## Finished papers

Sometimes newspapers are delivered to people's homes. They also can be bought at newsstands and in stores.

## Photo research

Researchers look for the right photo to go with a news story.

**Find Out More** on page 29

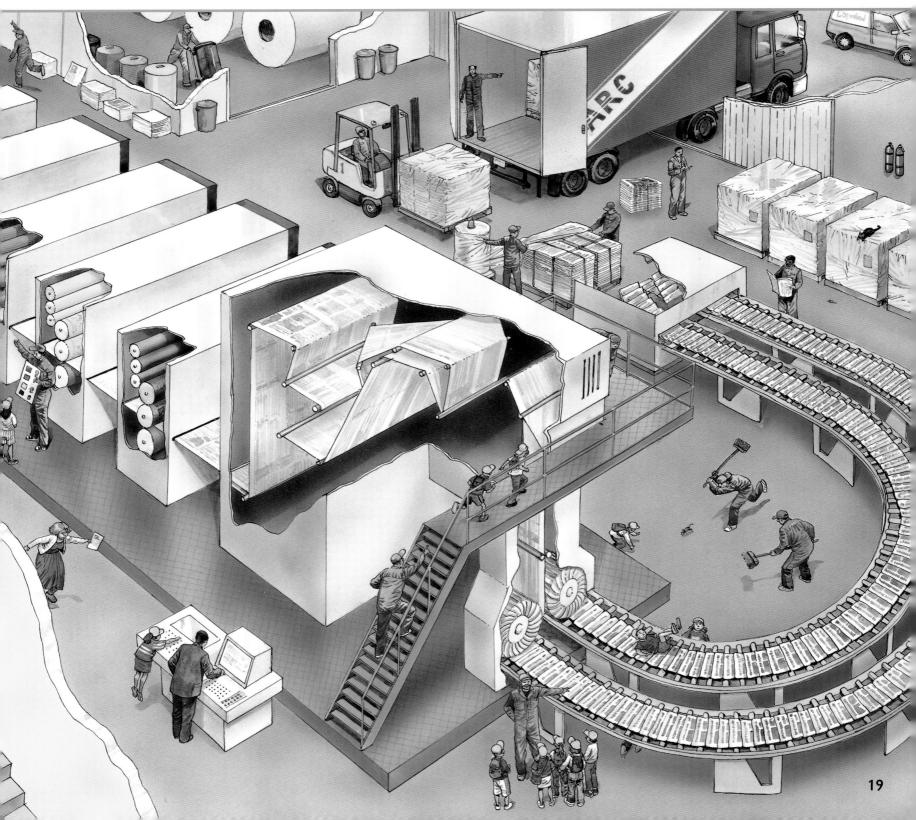

# Construction Site

It takes many workers and machines to construct a building. The chief builder must make sure that the building plans are followed. Some workers cut wood. Others mix, pour, and smooth concrete. Flatbed trucks deliver steel beams, and bulldozers move dirt. A construction site is a busy and noisy place!

## Search & Find

- ☐ Backhoe
- ☐ Cement mixers (2)
- ☐ Crane operator
- ☐ Ladders (5)
- ☐ Man walking in wet cement
- ☐ Men carrying a steel beam
- ☐ Telephone
- ☐ Wheelbarrows (5)

### Bulldozer
A bulldozer uses its large, metal shovel to move dirt and rocks.

### Flatbed truck
A flatbed truck has a long, flat surface. It is used to carry large or heavy things.

### Pile driver
A pile driver pounds long pieces of wood or steel into the ground.

### Carpenter
A carpenter builds things out of wood.

### Dump truck
A dump truck carries dirt or gravel and dumps it where it belongs.

### Architect
A person who designs a building is called an architect (AR-kuh-tekt).

### General contractor
This person hires all the workers needed to build the building. The general contractor makes sure that all the work is done right.

**Find Out More** on page 30

# Movie Set

Many movies are made in busy studios.
Costume designers make the actors' clothing.
Sound technicians (tek-NIH-shunz) work the microphones.
Special sets must be built. On the set, the actors perform.
The director tells them when to speak and where to move.
Lights, camera, action!

## Search & Find

- ☐ Bucket of water
- ☐ Cafeteria
- ☐ Chickens (8)
- ☐ Cowboy hat
- ☐ Dogs (2)
- ☐ Handkerchief
- ☐ Man ironing
- ☐ Parrot

**Find Out More**
on page 30

## Actors

An actor is a person who plays a character in a movie, television show, or play.

## Camera operator

The camera operator films the actors while they perform.

## Makeup artist

A makeup artists puts makeup on the actor's face.

## Sound crew

The sound crew records sound needed for the movie.

## Costume designers

Costume designers make the clothes the actors wear in the movie.

## Director

The director gives the actors directions about how to play their roles. The director is also in charge of the crew.

## Lighting

The lighting person controls how the set is lit. The set can be lit to look like day or night.

23

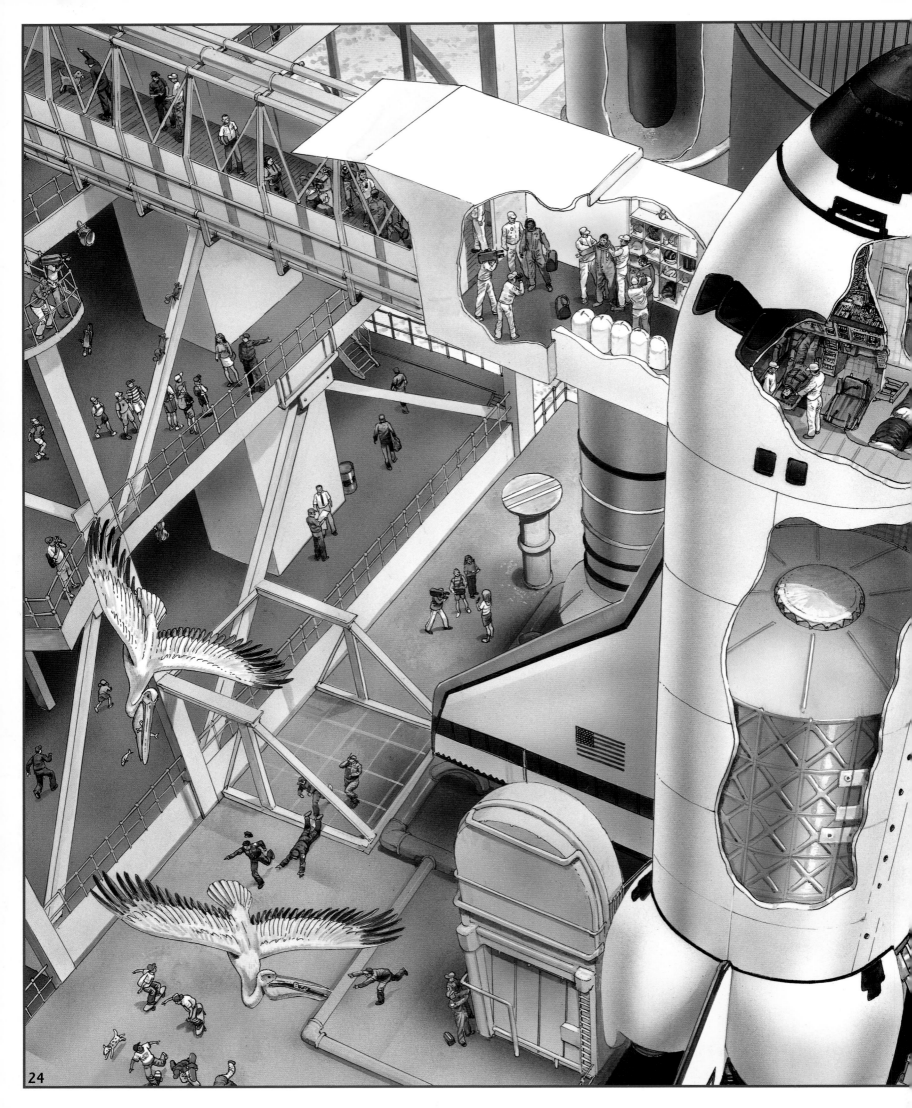

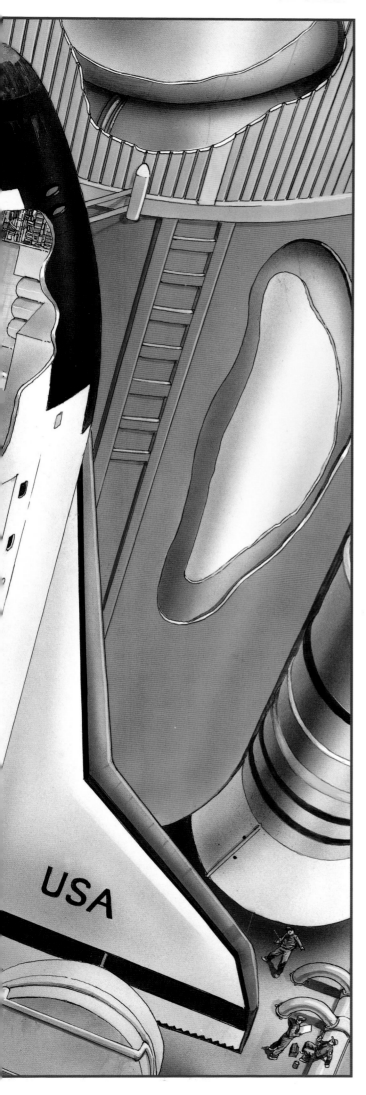

# Space Shuttle

"Three, two, one, blastoff!" Flying a shuttle into space is a big event. Engineers make sure that the shuttle is ready to go. The astronauts put on special flight suits and prepare for takeoff. Soon, powerful rocket engines will shoot the shuttle into space.

## Search & Find

- ☐ Dogs (2)
- ☐ Flag
- ☐ Man tripping
- ☐ Photographers (2)
- ☐ Skateboarders
- ☐ Squirrels (2)
- ☐ Tour guide
- ☐ Video cameras (4)

### Space shuttle
The space shuttle is a craft that carries people and cargo into space and back again.

### Payload bay
Cargo is stored in an area called the payload bay.

### Engineers
Engineers make sure that the shuttle is ready for its mission.

### Flight suit
An astronaut's flight suit is designed for safety. The suit comes with an oxygen supply, drinking water, a life raft, a parachute, and many other life-saving features.

### Film crew
The film crew records how the astronauts prepare for their flight.

### Bridge
Crew members and technicians enter the shuttle by crossing a bridge. The bridge is high above the ground.

**Find Out More** on page 31

## Find Out More

## Train Station

The first railroad track in the United States opened in 1830. It began at Baltimore harbor and was only 13 miles long.

The first steam engine in America was designed by Peter Cooper. It was called Tom Thumb. Tom Thumb could pull a train at six miles per hour. Modern trains can travel at almost 250 miles per hour!

The average freight train is made up of 100 cars.

Circus trains transport animals and equipment from place to place.

Many trains have special cars where people can sit and have a drink or a snack.

The ceiling of Grand Central Station in New York City is decorated with stars that twinkle.

The longest railway in the world is in Russia. It is almost 6,000 miles long!

### Learn more at:
www.trainmuseum.org

www.trains.com

# Harbor

Some seagulls drink seawater. The extra salt leaves their bodies through their nostrils.

The first lighthouse built in North America was the Boston Lighthouse. It was built in 1716.

For some people, a yacht or sailboat is their home.

**The word** *scuba* **is short for "self-contained underwater breathing apparatus."**

The word *kayak* comes from an Inuit (IH-nyoo-wut) word that means "man's boat."

Large ferries can carry trucks and trains as well as people.

Special shipping containers are used to transport fruit, vegetables, flowers, and dairy products. Fruit from South America can end up in a lunch box in Chicago.

## Learn more at:

**www.mariner.org**

**http://scubarangers.com**

**www.kids-fishing.com**

# Gas Station

A car wash uses less water than washing a car at home does. Also, at a car wash, the dirty water runs into a special tank instead of the ground.

Mechanics fix machines. The mechanics at this gas station are fixing cars.

Some gas stations stay open 24 hours a day, seven days a week.

Many stations have a convenience (kun-VEEN-yunce) store. This store sells food, drinks, maps, and many other things that travelers may need.

A bicycle-built-for-two is called a tandem (TAN-dum). It has two seats and two sets of pedals.

**Bicyclists need to obey the rules of the road just as drivers of cars, trucks, and motorcycles do.**

## Learn more at:

**http://vintagegas.com**

**http://volocars.com**

# Submarine

Small, movable fins on both sides of the submarine help it dive and rise to the surface.

Special tanks also help a submarine dive or surface. When the tanks are filled with sea water, the submarine gets heavier and sinks. When the seawater is forced out of the tanks and is replaced with air, the submarine gets lighter and rises.

Ship propellers usually have four to seven blades.

Submarine engines are built to make as little noise as possible.

**The giant squid's eyeball is the largest in the animal kingdom. It is about the size of a volleyball. The giant squid is a sperm whale's favorite food.**

Alvin is the name of a famous deep-sea submersible. It can dive to a depth of more than two and one-half miles.

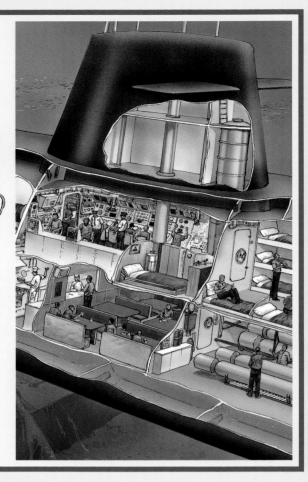

## Learn more at:

http://oceanexplorer.noaa.gov

www.bowfin.org

# Fire Station

**When people are trapped, firefighters use axes and crowbars to break open doors and windows.**

A fire extinguisher (ek-STING-gwi-shur) can be used to put out a small fire. It sprays foam instead of water.

Different fire trucks do different jobs. A pumper truck pumps water through the hoses. The tanker truck carries more than 1,000 gallons of water. The ladder truck has a very long ladder that helps firefighters climb to the top of tall buildings.

Years ago, firefighters traveled to fires on horse-drawn carriages. Dalmatian dogs guided the horses through streets filled with traffic. Dalmatians are still fire station mascots.

**A firefighter's uniform weighs nearly 60 pounds. It is waterproof and fireproof.**

Firefighters carry an oxygen tank on their back. The oxygen helps them breathe when they are fighting a fire.

## Learn more at:

http://nycfiremuseum.org

www.sparky.org

# Airport

A luggage cart takes people's bags to and from the airplane.

Most airports have restaurants and shops for travelers who are waiting to begin their trip.

In 1930, eight nurses became the first flight attendants to work on an airplane.

More than three billion people a year pass through the world's airports.

Air-traffic controllers speak to the pilots of airplanes that are waiting to take off or land. They make sure the planes move safely.

The first air-traffic controllers worked outside. They used flags to communicate with pilots.

Carry-on bags are x-rayed to see if they contain dangerous objects.

**Learn more at:**

http://faa.gov

www.nasm.si.edu

http://ninety-nines.org

# Newspaper Office

Printing presses print newspapers on large rolls of paper. Some presses can print more than 1,000 newspapers per minute.

Editors must decide which stories to print. The most important stories appear on the front page of a newspaper.

**Sometimes newspapers are printed using a combination of four ink colors: blue, red, yellow, and black.**

The first issue of America's first regular newspaper, the *Boston News–Letter*, was published on April 24, 1704.

**Trucks rush newspapers to stores and newsstands early in the morning.**

**Learn more at:**

http://kidsnewsroom.org

www.timeforkids.com

29

# Construction Site

Everyone at a construction site must wear a hard hat for safety.

**The concrete mixer spins to keep the concrete from getting hard. The soft concrete comes down a chute to where it is needed.**

Some construction machines, such as bulldozers, are taken to work sites on flatbed trucks.

**A backhoe has a shovel in front and a digger in the back. The digger is often used to dig trenches.**

**A bulldozer has metal crawler belts instead of wheels. The belts help it move over rough or soft ground without tipping over or sinking.**

## Learn more at:

www.kenkenkikki.jp

# Movie Set

**An extra is an actor with a small, background role in a movie.**

A boom is a long pole with a microphone on one end. Other names for the boom are giraffe and fishpole.

Early movies were filmed in black and white and had no sound. Often, a piano player in the theater provided music to go with the movie.

Indoor movie sets are built inside huge buildings. Set builders can create an ancient city, a tropical jungle, or any other place that you can imagine.

**The sound editor works on the film's sound track. A sound track is all of the music that goes along with a movie.**

## Learn more at:

www.cicff.org

# Space Shuttle

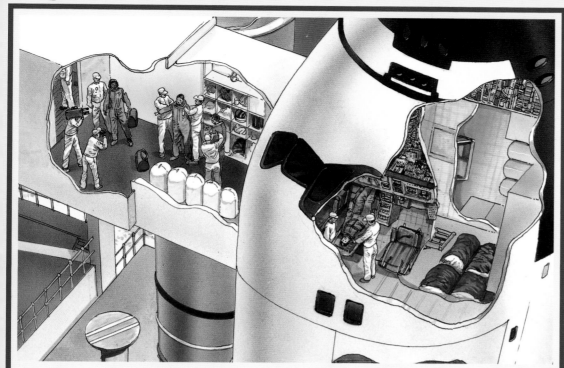

Learn more at:

**http://kidsastronomy.com**

**www.nasa.gov**

The space shuttle is mainly controlled by computers on the ground.

Out in space, a space shuttle circles Earth about once every 90 minutes. The crew can watch the sun rise or set every 45 minutes.

**A space shuttle can carry up to eight astronauts, including the commander and the pilot.**

Space shuttles are launched from the John F. Kennedy Space Center in Florida.

**The shuttle's cargo sometimes includes space probes or satellites.**

Space shuttle missions usually last about ten days. There is extra food, fuel, and water on board in case the shuttle can't return on time.

The space shuttle moves very fast. It goes from standing still just before takeoff to a speed of 17,000 miles per hour in about eight minutes.